Sous Vide Best Recipes

Over 50 Delicious Recipes For You Sous Vide Cooking

Alexa Jane

Table of Contents

BREAKFAST

1. Balsamic Mushroom & Herbs

Preparation Time: 15 minutes, Cooking time: 1 hour, Servings: 4

Ingredients

- 1-pound cremini mushrooms with the stems removed

- 1 tablespoon extra-virgin olive oil

- 1 tablespoon apple balsamic vinegar

- 1 minced garlic clove

- 1 teaspoon kosher salt

- 1 teaspoon freshly ground black pepper

- 1 teaspoon minced fresh thyme

Directions:

1. Prepare the Sous-vide water bath using your immersion circulator and raise the temperature to 138°F.

2. Add the listed ingredients to your resealable zip bag.

3. Seal using the immersion method and let it cook for 1 hour.

4. Once cooked, transfer the contents to a platter and serve!

Nutrition: Calories 414, Carbohydrates 51 g, Fats 18 g, Protein 12 g

2. Currant & Braised Cabbage

Preparation Time: 15 minutes, Cooking time: 2 hours, Servings: 4

Ingredients

- 1 ½ pounds red cabbage

- ¼ cup currants

- 1 thinly sliced shallot

- 3 thinly sliced garlic clove

- 1 tablespoon apple balsamic vinegar

- 1 tablespoon unsalted butter

- ½ a teaspoon kosher salt

Directions:

1. Prepare the Sous-vide water bath using your immersion circulator and raise the temperature to 185°F.

2. Take the cabbage and slice the cabbage into quarters, make sure to discard the core.

3. Chop them up into 1 ½-inch pieces.

4. Take 2 heavy-duty resealable zipper bags and divide the cabbages between the two bags.

5. Divide as well the remaining ingredients equally between the bags

11

6. Seal using the immersion method. Submerge underwater and cook for 2 hours.

7. Once done, remove the bag and transfer to a bowl.

8. Add the cooking juices and season with a bit of salt and vinegar.

9. Serve!

Nutrition: Calories 178, Carbohydrates 6 g, Fats 14 g, Protein 7 g

3. <u>Sous-vide Pennies</u>

Preparation Time: 15 minutes, Cooking time: 3 hours, Servings: 4

Ingredients

- 1-pound carrots, peeled up and sliced into ¼ inch thick rounds

- ¼ cup dried apricots, thinly sliced up

- ¼ cup freshly squeezed orange juice

- 2 tablespoons freshly squeezed lemon juice

- 1 tablespoon unsalted vegan butter

- 2 teaspoons beet sugar

- ½ a teaspoon kosher salt

- ¼ teaspoon orange zest

- ¼ teaspoon freshly ground black pepper

- 1/8 teaspoon ground cinnamon

Directions:

1. Prepare the Sous-vide water bath using your immersion circulator and raise the temperature to 183°F.

2. Add the listed ingredients to your resealable zip bag and seal using the immersion method. Submerge underwater and cook for 3 hours.

3. Transfer the carrots to a serving platter with cooking liquid and season with salt and pepper.

4. Garnish with the additional lemon juice and serve!

Nutrition: Calories 256, Carbohydrates 35 g, Fats 12 g, Protein 2 g

4. Pomme Purée

Preparation Time: 10 minutes, Cooking time: 30 minutes, Servings: 4

Ingredients

- 1½ lb. potatoes, peeled
- 15-ounce vegan butter
- 8-ounce coconut milk
- A pinch of salt
- White pepper

Directions:

1. Prepare your Sous-vide water bath using your immersion circulator and raise the temperature to 194°F.

2. Slice the potatoes to 1 cm thick slices

3. Take your heavy-duty resealable zipper bag and add the potatoes, coconut milk, vegan butter and salt

4. Submerge underwater and let it cook for 30 minutes

5. Strain the mixture through a metal mesh/sieve and allow the butter mixture to pour into a bowl

6. Puree the potatoes by blending them or mashing them using a spoon

7. Pour the puree into the butter bowl

8. Season with pepper and serve!

Nutrition: Calories 57, Carbohydrates 2 g, Fats 5 g, Protein 1 g

5. <u>Sous-vide Golden Beets</u>

Preparation Time: 20 minutes, Cooking time: 1 hour 30 minutes, Servings: 2

Ingredients

- 1 lb. golden beets, cut up into ¼ inch thick slices

- 1 cup freshly squeezed orange juice

- ¼ cup freshly squeezed lemon juice

- 4 tablespoons unsalted vegan butter

- 1 tablespoon agave nectar

- 1 teaspoon freshly ground black peppercorns

- 1 teaspoon kosher salt

Directions:

1. Prepare the Sous-vide water bath using your immersion circulator and raise the temperature to 180°F.

2. Add the listed ingredients to a resealable zip bag and seal using the immersion method. Cook for 1 ½ hours

3. Once done, remove the bag and take the beets out and set them aside.

4. Pour the cooking liquid into a saucepan and bring it to a simmer over medium-high heat.

5. Keep simmering until the liquid is lowered by half.

6. Remove from the heat and stir in beets.

7. Serve!

Nutrition: Calories 176, Carbohydrates 7 g, Fats 16 g, Protein 1 g

6. <u>Fingerling Cooked Potatoes</u>

Preparation Time: 10 minutes, Cooking time: 45 minutes, Servings: 3

Ingredients

- 8 ounces fingerling potatoes

- Salt, and pepper to taste

- 1 tablespoon unsalted vegan butter

- 1 sprig rosemary

Directions:

1. Prepare the Sous-vide water bath using your immersion circulator and raise the temperature to 178°F.

2. Take the potatoes and season it with salt and pepper and transfer them to a resealable zip bag.

3. Seal using the immersion method and submerge it underwater and cook for 45 minutes.

4. Once cooked, remove the bag and potatoes.

5. Cut the potatoes in half (lengthwise).

6. Take a large skillet and put it over medium-high heat.

7. Add the butter and allow it to melt, add the rosemary and potatoes.

8. Cook for 3 minutes and transfer to a plate.

9. Serve by seasoning it with a bit of salt if needed

Nutrition: Calories 150, Carbohydrates 19 g, Fats 6 g, Protein 5 g

7. <u>Daikon Radishes</u>

Preparation Time: 10 minutes, Cooking time: 30 minutes, Servings: 4

Ingredients

- ½ cup white winger vinegar

- 3 tablespoons beet sugar

- 2 teaspoons kosher salt

- 1 large size Daikon radish, trimmed and sliced up

Directions:

1. Prepare the Sous-vide water bath using your immersion circulator and raise the temperature to 180°F.

2. Take a large bowl and mix in vinegar, salt, and beet sugar.

3. Transfer to a Sous-vide zip bag and seal using the immersion method.

4. Submerge underwater and cook for 30 minutes

5. Once cooked, remove the bag and transfer to an ice bath.

6. Serve!

Nutrition: Calories 166, Carbohydrates 19 g, Fats 6 g, Protein 9 g

8. <u>Green Beans in Tomato Sauce</u>

Preparation Time: 10 minutes, Cooking time: 3 hours, Servings: 4

Ingredients

- 1 lb. trimmed green beans

- 1 can whole crushed tomatoes

- 1 thinly sliced onion

- 3 garlic cloves, peeled and thinly sliced

- Kosher salt, to taste

- Extra-virgin olive oil

Directions:

1. Prepare the Sous-vide water bath using your immersion circulator and raise the temperature to 183°F

2. Take a large heavy-duty resealable zip bag and add the tomatoes, green beans, garlic, and onion

3. Seal using the immersion method. Submerge underwater and let it cook for 3 hours.

4. Once cooked, transfer the contents of the bag to a large bowl.

5. Serve with a seasoning of salt and a drizzle of olive oil.

Nutrition: Calories 275, Carbohydrates 6 g, Fats 19 g, Protein 20 g

9. <u>French Fries</u>

Preparation Time: 20 minutes, Cooking time: 25 minutes, Servings: 10

Ingredients

- 2 quarts' water

- 2 tablespoons kosher salt

- 1 teaspoon beet sugar

- 1 teaspoon baking powder

- 2 ½ pounds russet potatoes, cut up into French fry shapes

Directions:

1. Prepare the Sous-vide water bath using your immersion circulator and raise the temperature to 194°F.

2. Take a large bowl and add the water, sugar, kosher salt, and baking powder.

3. Give everything a nice mix until everything dissolves.

4. Add the sliced-up potatoes to the mixture and transfer it to a heavy-duty resealable zipper bag.

5. Seal using the immersion method. Submerge underwater and let it cook for 25 minutes.

6. Once done, remove the bag and pre-heat your Air Fryer to a temperature of 260°F.

7. Let the fries cool for 20 minutes and Air Fry them for 8 minutes.

8. Transfer them to a freezer and let them chill for 60 minutes.

9. Preheat your fryer to 735°F and cook them again for 2 minutes.

10. Serve!

Nutrition: Calories 345, Carbohydrates 67 g , Fats 5 g, Protein 8 g

10. Moroccan Chickpeas

Preparation Time: 10 minutes, Cooking time: 3 hours, Servings: 4

Ingredients

- 1 cup chickpeas, soaked overnight in cold salty water

- 3 cups water

- 2 tablespoons extra-virgin olive oil

- 1 teaspoon kosher salt

- ½ teaspoon ground cumin

- ½ teaspoon ground coriander

- ¼ teaspoon ground cinnamon

- 1/8 teaspoon ground cloves

- 1/8 teaspoon cayenne pepper

- Fresh cilantro for garnishing, chopped

- Harissa, to taste

Directions:

Prepare the Sous-vide water bath using your immersion circulator and increase the temperature to 190°F.

1. Then, drain the soaked chickpeas and transfer them to a resealable bag with the soaking water

2. Add in the cumin, salt, olive oil, cloves, cinnamon, coriander, and cayenne pepper.

3. Seal using the immersion method. Submerge underwater and let it cook for 3 hours.

4. Drain the chickpeas from the liquid and transfer them to a bowl.

5. Season with a bit of salt.

6. Take a small bowl and add the olive oil and harissa.

7. Drizzle the mixture over the chickpeas.

8. Serve with a garnish of cilantro.

Nutrition: Calories 189, Carbohydrates 29 g, Fats 5 g, Protein 7 g

11.   Pickle in A Jar

Preparation Time: 30 minutes, Cooking time: 15 minutes, Servings: 6

Ingredients

- 1 cup white wine vinegar
- ½ cup beet sugar
- 2 teaspoons kosher salt
- 1 tablespoon pickling spice
- 2 English cucumbers sliced up into ¼ inch thick slices
- ½ white onion, thinly sliced

Directions:

1. Prepare the Sous-vide water bath using your immersion circulator and raise the temperature to 180°F.

2. Take a large bowl and add the vinegar, sugar, salt, pickling spice and whisk them well.

3. Transfer to a heavy-duty resealable zipper bag alongside the cucumber and sliced onions and seal using the immersion method.

4. Submerge underwater and let it cook for 15 minutes.

5. Transfer the bag to an ice bath

6. Pour the mixture into a 4-6-ounce mason jar

7. Serve or store!

Nutrition: Calories 121, Carbohydrates 27 g, Fats 1 g, Protein 1 g

12.   Sous Vide Glazed Carrots

Preparation Time: 4 minutes, Cooking time: 20 minutes, Servings: 3

Ingredients:

- 4-5 carrots of different colors, peeled, sliced

- ½ cup of chopped pumpkin or sweet potato

- 1 tsp of dried thyme

- 1 tbsp of salted butter

- Salt/Pepper

Directions:

1. Prepare your Sous Vide water bath by attaching the immersion circulator and setting the temperature to 194°F.

2. Place the carrots in a pouch and seal using the vacuum sealer or the water displacement method.

3. Let cook in the water bath for 25 minutes.

4. Remove the carrots from the pouch and glaze in a pan with the butter and thyme until they get a sleek golden sheen and serve

Nutrition: Calories 98, Carbohydrates 14.7 g, Protein 1.73 g, Fats 6 g

13.   Eggplant Parmesan

Preparation Time: 5 minutes, Cooking time: 1 hour, Servings: 2

Ingredients:

- 1 large eggplant, sliced

- 2 large eggs, beaten

- ¼ cup parmesan cheese, grated

- 1 cup, tomato sauce

- ½ cup, bread crumbs

- ⅓ cup, white flour

- 4 tablespoons olive oil

- Salt/pepper

Directions:

1. Prepare your Sous Vide water bath by attaching the immersion circulator and setting the temperature to 183°F.

2. Place the eggplants on water, pinch with a fork and let them release their bitterness in the water for 10 minutes. Drain, season with salt, pepper, and set aside.

3. Place and distribute the eggplant slices into 2-3 pouches, while these are lying flat. Seal using the water displacement method or the vacuum sealer (while placing the pouch horizontally so that eggplants are not on top of each other).

4. Submerge into the water and let cook for 40 minutes.

5. In three separate small bowls, divide the beaten eggs, the breadcrumbs, and the flour. Season everything with salt and pepper.

6. Once the eggplants are cooked, dip each slice into the flour, then to the eggs and then to the breadcrumb mixture.

7. Heat the olive oil in a medium pan (over medium heat) and place the breaded eggplant slices. Cook for 2-3 minutes on each side, or until golden brown.

8. Transfer the eggplants into a baking dish or pyrex and pour over the tomato sauce and the grated mozzarella cheese.

9. Pop these into the oven and cook for 15-20 minutes (or until cheese is melted)

10. Serve hot

Nutrition: Calories 679.9, Carbohydrates 66.5 g, Fats 39.1 g, Protein 15.5 g

14.   Sous Vide Balsamic Onions

Preparation Time: 3 minutes, Cooking time: 2 hours, Servings: 2

Ingredients:

- 2 medium white onions, sliced julienne

- 1 tbsp, balsamic vinegar

- 2 tbsp, brown sugar

- 2 tbsp, olive oil

- Salt/Pepper to taste

Directions:

1. Prepare your Sous Vide water bath by attaching the immersion circulator and setting the temperature to 185°F.

2. Mix the onions with the rest of the ingredients in a sealable plastic bag and seal using a vacuum sealer or the water displacement method.

3. Submerge into the bath water and allow cooking for 2 hours.

4. Remove, transfer into a mason jar, cool and keep in the fridge for up to 12 hours before serving.

Nutrition: Calories 186.7, Carbohydrates 15.5 g, Fats 13.5 g, Protein 0.8 g

15. Sous Vide Turmeric and Cumin

Tofu

Preparation Time: 5 minutes, Cooking time: 2 hours, Servings: 4

Ingredients:

- 1 pack, firm tofu, drained and cut to ½ inch thick pieces

- 3 cloves, garlic, minced

- 1 tbsp, turmeric

- 1 tsp, cumin

- 2 tbsp, lime

- 3 tablespoons olive oil

- Kosher salt/Pepper

Directions:

1. Prepare your Sous Vide water bath by attaching the immersion circulator and setting the temperature to 180°F.

2. Arrange the tofu pieces on a flat surface (you can use a baking tray) and place on the fridge for 15 minutes.

3. In a small bowl, combine all the rest of the ingredients to make a marinade.

4. Take the tofu pieces out of the fridge and dip into the marinade, making sure all pieces are well coated.

5. Transfer the marinated tofu on a sealable pouch (lying flat) and seal using a vacuum sealer or the water displacement method.

6. Submerge into the water bath and let cook for 2 hours.

7. Take out of the pouch carefully and serve as it is or with lettuce or Roca leaves as a garnish.

Nutrition: Calories 220, Carbohydrates 5.4 g, Fats 16.9 g, Protein 11.7 g

16.   Garlic Mushrooms with Truffle Oil

Preparation Time: 5 minutes, Cooking time: 1 hour, Servings: 2

Ingredients:

- 10 mediums to large button mushrooms

- 2 cloves, garlic, minced

- 3 tbsp, olive oil

- 2 tbsp of truffle oil

- 1 tbsp of fresh thyme, chopped

- Salt/Pepper

Directions:

1. Prepare your Sous Vide water bath by attaching the immersion circulator and setting the temperature to 185°F.

2. Mix the olive oil with the truffle oil and the rest of the ingredients. Add the mushrooms and make sure that they are well coated with the oil mixture.

3. Place the mushrooms into a sealable plastic pouch and seal using a vacuum sealer or the water displacement method.

4. Place into the water bath and cook for 1 hour.

5. Once the mushrooms are cooked, remove from the bag, drain and toss in a grilling pan to sear, until golden brown.

6. Serve hot and garnish optionally with some extra thyme on top.

Nutrition: Calories 330, Carbohydrates 4.4 g, Fats 34.1 g, Protein 1.5 g

17. Green Chicken Salad With Almonds

Preparation Time: 95 minutes

Cooking Time: 25-75 minutes

Servings: 2

Ingredients:

- 2 chicken breasts, skinless

- Salt and black pepper to taste

- 1 cup almonds

- 1 tbsp olive oil

- 2 tbsp sugar

- 4 red chilis, thinly sliced

- 1 garlic clove, peeled

- 3 tbsp fish sauce

- 2 tsp freshly squeezed lime juice

- 1 cup cilantro, chopped

- 1 scallion, thinly sliced

- 1 stalk lemongrass, white part only, sliced

- 1 piece 2-inch ginger, julienned

Directions:

1. Prepare a water bath and place the Sous Vide in it. Set to 138 F. Place the chicken seasoned with salt and pepper in a vacuum-sealable bag. Release air by the water displacement method, seal and submerge the bag in the water bath. Cook for 75 minutes.

2. After 60 minutes, heat the olive oil in a saucepan to 350 F. Toast the almonds for 1 minute until dry. Batter the sugar, garlic and chili. Pour the fish sauce and lime juice.

3. Once the timer has stopped, remove the bag and allow cooling. Chop the chicken in bites and place into a bowl. Pour the dressing and mix well. Add the cilantro, ginger, lemongrass and fried cashews. Combine well. Garnish with chili.

Nutrition: Calories 352, Fat 5, Fiber 3, Carbs 7, Protein 5

LUNCH

18. Lamb Leg Steak with Chimichurri

Preparation Time: 15 minutes, Cooking time: 6 hours, Servings: 4

Ingredients:

- 4 5oz. lamb leg steaks

- 4 tablespoons butter

- Salt and pepper, to taste

- Chimichurri:

- 1 bunch fresh parsley, chopped

- ½ bunch fresh mint, chopped

- 1 bunch fresh basil, chopped

- 2 cloves garlic, chopped

- 1 teaspoon salt

- 1-inch minced ginger

- 2 red chili peppers, seeded, chopped

- ¾ cup olive oil

- ¼ cup vinegar

- ¼ cup water

- 1 lime, juiced

- 1 splash soy sauce

Directions:

1. Preheat Sous Vide cooker to 140°F.

2. Season lamb steaks with salt and pepper. Place the lamb steaks and butter into Sous Vide bags. Vacuum seal.

3. Cook the lamb 6 hours.

4. Make the chimichurri; in a bowl, combine all the chimichurri ingredients. Stir well.

5. Remove the lamb from the bag and pat dry.

6. Sear in a very hot skillet until browned on all sides.

7. Serve warm with chimichurri.

Nutrition: Calories 740, Carbohydrates 33.2 g, Fats 53.9 g, Protein 30.6 g

19.   Lamb Shoulder with Vegetables

Preparation Time: 10 minutes, Cooking time: 14 hours, Servings: 4

Ingredients:

- 3lb. lamb shoulder

- 1 cup beef stock

- 4 tablespoons olive oil

- 2 sprigs thyme

- Vegetables:

- 1 zucchini, trimmed, sliced

- 2 red bell peppers, seeded, quartered

- 3 sprigs parsley

- 1 tablespoon olive oil

- 1 clove garlic

- Salt and pepper, to taste

- 1 tablespoon butter

Directions:

1. Preheat Sous Vide cooker to 155°F.

2. Remove any fat from the lamb and season generously with salt and pepper.

3. Heat some oil in a skillet.

4. Sear the lamb shoulder in a large skillet and transfer into Sous Vide cooking bag.

5. Add the beef stock, remaining olive oil, and thyme. Vacuum seal the lamb and

   submerge in water.

6. Cook the lamb 14 hours.

7. Make the vegetables; melt butter in a skillet.

8. Add garlic and cook 30 seconds. Add the bell peppers and cook 3 minutes.

9. Toss in the remaining ingredients and cook 3 minutes. Place aside.

10. Remove the lamb from the cooking bag. Using a torch create a brown crust on the lamb.

11. Serve lamb with prepared veggies.

Nutrition: Calories 569, Carbohydrates 26.8 g, Fats 37.8 g, Protein 30.3 g

20.   Beef Wellington

Preparation Time: 1 hour, Cooking time: 2 hours, Servings: 4

Ingredients

- 1 lb. beef tenderloin fillet

- Salt and pepper

- 2 tablespoons Dijon mustard

- 1 sheet puff pastry, thawed

- 8 oz. cremini mushrooms

- 1 shallot, diced

- 3 cloves garlic, chopped

- 1 tablespoon unsalted butter

- 6 slices prosciutto

Directions:

1. Prepare the Sous Vide water bath using your immersion circulator and raise the temperature to 124°F

2. Take the beef tenderloin and generously season it with pepper and salt

3. Place in a zip bag and seal using the immersion method. Cook for 2 hours

4. Chop the mushrooms in a food processor, put the shallots and garlic in a hot pan

5. Cook until tender, add the chopped mushrooms and cook until water has evaporated

6. Add 1 tablespoon of butter and cook

7. Once done, remove the beef from the bag and pat dry

8. Heat the oil in a cast iron pan until shimmering. Sear the beef on all sides for 30 seconds

9. Spread the Dijon mustard all over the tenderloin

10. Lay a plastic wrap on a surface and arrange your prosciutto slices horizontally. Spread the Duxelles thinly over the prosciutto and place the tenderloin on top

11. Roll the tender loin in the plastic wrap tightly and chill for 20 minutes

12. Roll out your thawed pastry and brush with egg wash. Unwrap the tender loin and place in the pastry puff

13. Bake for 10 minutes in your oven at 475°F, slice and serve!

Nutrition: Calories 342, Carbohydrates 11 g, Fats 22 g, Protein 25 g

DINNER

21.   **Pesto Turkey**

Preparation time: 10 minutes

Cooking time: 50 minutes

Servings: 4

Ingredients:

- 1 pound turkey breasts, skinless, boneless and cubed
- ½ cup chicken stock
- 1 tablespoon basil pesto
- 1 tablespoon lime juice
- 2 tablespoons olive oil
- 1 teaspoon chili powder
- A pinch of salt and black pepper
- 1 tablespoon chives, chopped

Directions:

1. In a large sous vide bag, mix the turkey with the stock, pesto and the other ingredients, seal the bag and cook in the water bath at 180 degrees F for 50 minutes.

2. Divide everything between plates and serve.

Nutrition: calories 16 fat 8 fiber 2 carbs 5 protein 9

22.　Mustard Chicken and Capers

Preparation time: 10 minutes

Cooking time: 50 minutes

Servings: 4

Ingredients:

- 2 tablespoons avocado oil

- 2 pounds chicken breasts, skinless, boneless and cut into strips

- 1 tablespoon capers, drained

- 3 scallions minced

- 1 tablespoon mustard

- 1 tablespoon lime zest, grated

- Juice 1 lime

- ¾ cup chicken stock

- A pinch of salt and black pepper

- 1 tablespoon parsley, chopped

Directions:

1. In a large sous vide bag, mix the chicken with the oil, capers and the other ingredients, seal the bag and cook in the water bath at 180 degrees F for 50 minutes.

2. Divide the mix between plates and serve.

Nutrition: calories 200 fat 9 fiber 2 carbs 5 protein 10

23.   Orange Chicken Mix

Preparation time: 10 minutes

Cooking time: 2 hours

Servings: 4

Ingredients:

- 1 pound chicken breast, skinless, boneless and roughly cubed

- 1 cup orange, peeled and cut into segments

- 1 tablespoon avocado oil

- 1 cup orange juice

- 1 tablespoon chives, chopped

- A pinch of salt and black pepper

Directions:

1. In a large sous vide bag, mix the chicken with the orange, oil and the other ingredients, toss, seal the bag, submerge in the water bath and cook at 175 degrees F for 2 hours.

2. Divide the mix into bowls and serve.

Nutrition: calories 200 fat 7 fiber 2 carbs 6 protein 11

24.   Turkey with Sauce

Preparation time: 10 minutes

Cooking time: 1 hour

Servings: 4

Ingredients:

- 1 cup heavy cream
- 1 tablespoon olive oil
- 1 red onion, sliced
- ½ teaspoon garam masala
- 1 red chili, minced
- 1 teaspoon sweet paprika
- ½ cup chives, chopped
- 1 pound turkey breasts, skinless, boneless and cubed
- 1 tablespoon mustard
- 1 tablespoon lime zest, grated

Directions:

1. In a large sous vide bag, combine the turkey with the mustard, cream and the other ingredients, toss, seal the bag, submerge in the water bath, cook at 170 degrees F for 1 hour, divide the mix between plates and serve.

Nutrition: calories 210 fat 8 fiber 2 carbs 6 protein 11

25. Italian Turkey and Carrots

Preparation time: 10 minutes

Cooking time: 1 hour

Servings: 4

Ingredients:

- 1 pound turkey breast, skinless, boneless and roughly cubed

- ½ pound baby carrots, peeled

- 1 cup chicken stock

- 1 tablespoon avocado oil

- 1 teaspoon Italian seasoning

- ½ teaspoon rosemary, dried

- ½ teaspoon turmeric powder

- A pinch of salt and black pepper

- 1 tablespoon cilantro, chopped

Directions:

1. Divide the turkey, carrots, stock and the other ingredients into 4 sous vide bags and seal them.

2. Submerge in the water bath, cook at 170 degrees F for 1 hour, divide between plates and serve.

Nutrition: calories 220 fat 8 fiber 2 carbs 5 protein 11

26.   Chicken and Green Beans

Preparation time: 10 minutes

Cooking time: 1 hour

Servings: 4

Ingredients:

- 1 red onion, chopped

- 1 cup tomato passata

- 2 tablespoons olive oil

- Salt and black pepper to the taste

- 1 tablespoon cilantro, chopped

- 1 pound chicken breasts, skinless, boneless and cut into strips

- 2 cups green beans, trimmed and halved

- 1 teaspoon curry powder

- ½ teaspoon chili powder

- ½ teaspoon rosemary, dried

Directions:

1.   Divide the chicken, green beans, curry powder and the other ingredients into 2 sous vide bags, seal them, submerge in the water bath, cook at 170 degrees F for 1 hour, divide the mix between plates and serve.

Nutrition: calories 192 fat 12 fiber 3 carbs 5 protein 12

27. Duck and Tomatoes

Preparation time: 10 minutes

Cooking time: 1 hour and 10 minutes

Servings: 4

Ingredients:

- 1 pound duck breasts, skinless, boneless and cubed

- 1 cup cherry tomatoes, halved

- ½ cup chicken stock

- Juice of 1 lime

- ½ teaspoon chili powder

- ½ teaspoon cumin, ground

- 2 tablespoons olive oil

- ½ teaspoon coriander, ground

- ½ teaspoon turmeric powder

- 1 tablespoon chives, chopped

Directions:

1. In a sous vide bag, mix the duck with the tomatoes, stock and the other ingredients, seal the bag and cook in the water bath at 170 degrees F for 1 hour and 10 minutes.

2. Divide the mix between plates and serve.

Nutrition: calories 200 fat 7 fiber 1 carbs 5 protein 12

28.   Garlic Chicken Mix

Preparation time: 10 minutes

Cooking time: 1 hour

Servings: 4

Ingredients:

- 1 pound chicken breast, skinless, boneless and cubed

- 1 tablespoon olive oil

- 4 garlic cloves, minced

- Juice of 1 lime

- ½ teaspoon coriander, ground

- 3 scallions, chopped

- A pinch of salt and black pepper

- 1 tablespoon parsley, chopped

Directions:

1. In a sous vide bag, mix the chicken with the oil, garlic and the other ingredients, seal the bag and cook in the water bath at 170 degrees F for 1 hour.

2. Divide the mix between plates and serve.

Nutrition: calories 231 fat 7 fiber 2 carbs 6 protein 12

29. Chicken and Avocado

Preparation time: 10 minutes

Cooking time: 45 minutes

Servings: 4

Ingredients:

- 1 pound chicken breast, skinless, boneless and cubed

- 1 cup avocado, peeled, pitted and cubed

- 1 tablespoon olive oil

- Juice of 1 lime

- 2 scallions, chopped

- ½ teaspoon sweet paprika

- ½ teaspoon chili powder

- A pinch of salt and black pepper

- 1 tablespoon chives, chopped

Directions:

1. In a sous vide bag, mix the chicken with the avocado, oil and the other ingredients, seal the bag, submerge in the water bath and cook at 180 degrees F for 45 minutes.

2. Divide everything between plates and serve.

Nutrition: calories 252 fat 12 fiber 4 carbs 7 protein 13

30.   Turkey and Tomato Sauce

Preparation time: 10 minutes

Cooking time: 1 hour

Servings: 4

Ingredients:

- 1 red onion, chopped

- 2 tablespoons olive oil

- A pinch of salt and black pepper

- 1 cup tomato passata

- 1 tablespoon chives, chopped

- 1 pound turkey breasts, skinless, boneless and cubed

- 1 carrot, sliced

- 1 parsnip, sliced

- Juice of 1 lime

Directions:

1. In a sous vide bag, combine the turkey with the carrot, parsnip and the other ingredients, seal the bag, submerge into preheated water bath and cook at 175 degrees F for 1 hour.

2. Divide everything between plates and serve.

Nutrition: calories 221 fat 14 fiber 3 carbs 7 protein 14

31.   Turkey Medley

Preparation time: 10 minutes

Cooking time: 1 hour

Servings: 4

Ingredients:

- 1 eggplant, cubed

- 1 cup green beans, trimmed and halved

- 2 tablespoons balsamic vinegar

- A handful cilantro, chopped

- A pinch of salt and black pepper

- 1 pound turkey breast, skinless, boneless and cut into strips

- 1 tablespoon olive oil

- ½ cup white wine

- 2 scallions, chopped

- 1 cup black olives, pitted and halved

Directions:

1. In a large sous vide bag, combine the turkey with the oil, wine, scallions and the other ingredients, seal, submerge in the water oven and cook at 176 degrees F for 1 hour.

2. Divide the mix between plates and serve.

Nutrition: calories 263 fat 14 fiber 1 carbs 8 protein 12

32.   Chicken and Mango Mix

Preparation time: 10 minutes

Cooking time: 1 hour

Servings: 4

Ingredients:

- 1 teaspoon garam masala

- ½ teaspoon turmeric powder

- 1 tablespoon chives, chopped

- A pinch of salt and black pepper

- 1 pound chicken breast, skinless, boneless and sliced

- 1 cup mango, peeled and cubed

- 1 tablespoon olive oil

- Juice of 1 lime

Directions:

1. In a sous vide bag, mix the chicken with the mango, oil and the other ingredients, seal the bag, submerge in the water oven and cook at 190 degrees F for 1 hour.

2. Divide the mix between plates and serve.

Nutrition: calories 253 fat 13 fiber 2 carbs 7 protein 16

SNACKS

33. __Tuna Bites__

Preparation time: 15 minutes

Cooking time: 30 minutes

Servings: 6

Ingredients:

- 1 pound tuna fillets, boneless and roughly cubed

- 1 tablespoon olive oil

- 1 tablespoon soy sauce

- 1 teaspoon chili powder

- ½ teaspoon dill, dried

- 1 tablespoon parsley, chopped

- Salt and black pepper to the taste

Directions:

1. In a sous vide bag, combine the tuna with the oil, soy sauce and the other ingredients, toss, seal, submerge in the preheated water oven and cook at 130 degrees F for 30 minutes.

2. Arrange the tuna bites on a platter and serve them as an appetizer.

Nutrition: calories 170, fat 2, fiber 1, carbs 6, protein 6

34.   Shrimp and Cucumber Salad

Preparation time: 10 minutes

Cooking time: 30 minutes

Servings: 4

Ingredients:

- 3 cucumbers, cut with a spiralizer

- ½ cup mint, chopped

- 2 pounds shrimp, peeled and deveined

- 1 cup black olives, pitted and halved

- 1 tablespoon olive oil

- Salt and black pepper to the taste

- 2 tablespoons lime juice

- 2 teaspoons chili garlic sauce

- 1 tablespoon chives, chopped

Directions:

1. In a sous vide bag, combine the shrimp with the cucumbers, mint and the other ingredients, toss, seal the bag, submerge it in your preheated water oven and cook at 140 degrees F for 30 minutes.

2. Divide into bowls and serve.

Nutrition: calories 150, fat 2, fiber 3, carbs 6, protein 6

35. Lemon Mussels

Preparation time: 5 minutes

Cooking time: 20 minutes

Servings: 4

Ingredients:

- 2 pounds mussels, debearded and scrubbed

- ½ teaspoon rosemary, dried

- ½ teaspoon sweet paprika

- 1 tablespoon butter, melted

- 1 tablespoon lemon juice

Directions:

1. Put the mussels in a sous vide bag, add the rosemary and the other ingredients, seal the bag, submerge in the preheated water oven and cook at 194 degrees F for 20 minutes.

2. Arrange mussels on a platter, and serve.

Nutrition: calories 100, fat 1, fiber 1, carbs 6, protein 2

36.   Squid Salad

Preparation time: 10 minutes

Cooking time: 2 hours

Servings: 2

Ingredients:

- 1 pound squid, cut into medium rings

- 1 cup cherry tomatoes, halved

- 1 cup kalamata olives, pitted and halved

- 1 cup zucchinis, cubed

- 2 tablespoons olive oil

- 1 tablespoon balsamic vinegar

- A pinch of cayenne pepper

- Salt and black pepper to the taste

- 1 tablespoons lemon juice

- 1 tablespoon chives, chopped

- 1 teaspoon sriracha sauce

Directions:

1. In a sous vide bag, combine the squid rings with the tomatoes, olives and the
   other ingredients, toss, seal, submerge in the preheated water oven and cook at
   136 degrees F for 2 hours.

2. Divide the salad into bowls and serve.

Nutrition: calories 245, fat 32, fiber 3, carbs 12, protein 17

37. Calamari and Radish Salad

Preparation time: 10 minutes

Cooking time: 2 hours

Servings: 4

Ingredients:

- 2 cups calamari rings

- 1 cup radishes, sliced

- 1 cup kalamata olives, pitted and halved

- 1 tablespoon olive oil

- Juice of 1 lime

- A splash of Worcestershire sauce

- Salt and black pepper to the taste

- ½ teaspoon turmeric powder

- 1 tablespoon chives, chopped

Directions:

1. In a sous vide bag, combine the calamari with the radishes and the other ingredients, seal the bag, submerge in the preheated water oven and cook at 145 degrees F for 2 hours.

2. Divide into bowls and serve as an appetizer.

Nutrition: calories 368, fat 23, fiber 3, carbs 10, protein 34

38.   Octopus and Mango Salad

Preparation time: 10 minutes

Cooking time: 5 hours

Servings: 2

Ingredients:

- 2 pounds octopus, rinsed

- 1 cup mango, peeled and cubed

- 1 cup cherry tomatoes, halved

- 1 cup black olives, pitted and halved

- 1 cup cucumber, cubed

- 1 tablespoon balsamic vinegar

- 4 tablespoons olive oil

- 1 tablespoon chives, chopped

- Juice of 1 lemon

- Salt and black pepper to the taste

- 2 tablespoons parsley, chopped

Directions:

1. Put the octopus in a sous vide bag, drizzle half of the oil over it, season with salt and pepper, seal the bag, submerge it in the preheated water oven and cook at 170 degrees F for 5 hours.

2. Chop octopus, transfer to a bowl, add the rest of the ingredients, toss, divide into bowls and serve.

Nutrition: calories 200, fat 10, fiber 3, carbs 6, protein 23

39.   Clam Bowls

Preparation time: 10 minutes

Cooking time: 20 minutes

Servings: 4

Ingredients:

- 1 cup shallots, chopped

- 1 cup corn

- 1 cup kalamata olives, pitted and halved

- Juice of 1 lime

- ½ teaspoon chili powder

- Salt and black pepper to the taste

- 1 cup chicken stock

- 14 ounces baby clams

- 1 cup heavy cream

- 1 cup onion, chopped

- 1 tablespoon chives, chopped

Directions:

1. Put the clams in a sous vide bag, add salt, pepper and the stock, seal the bag, submerge it in the preheated water oven and cook at 190 degrees F for 20 minutes.

2. Open the clams, transfer the meat to a bowl, add the rest of the ingredients, toss, divide between plates and serve.

Nutrition: calories 220, fat 12, fiber 7, carbs 8, protein 13

40.   Italian Shrimp Salad

Preparation time: 10 minutes

Cooking time: 30 minutes

Servings: 4

Ingredients:

- 2 tablespoons avocado oil
- 1 cup pineapple, peeled and cubed
- 1 cup avocado, peeled, pitted and cubed
- 1 cup radishes, cubed
- 1 pound shrimp, peeled and deveined
- Salt and black pepper to the taste
- 2 tablespoons lime juice
- 2 teaspoons mint, chopped
- 1 tablespoon tarragon, chopped
- 1 tablespoon lemon juice
- 1 teaspoon lime zest, grated
- ½ cup heavy cream

Directions:

1. In a sous vide bag, combine the shrimp with the oil, pineapple and the other ingredients, seal the bag, submerge it in the preheated water oven and cook at 140 degrees F for 30 minutes.

2. Divide small bowls and serve as an appetizer.

Nutrition: calories 180, fat 11, fiber 2, carbs 8, protein 13

DESSERTS

41.   <u>Mango and Radishes Mix</u>

Preparation time: 10 minutes

Cooking time: 40 minutes

Servings: 4

Ingredients:

- 1 tablespoon balsamic vinegar

- ½ teaspoon chili powder

- 2 scallions, chopped

- Salt and black pepper to the taste

- 1 tablespoon chives, chopped

- 1 pound radishes, halved

- 1 cup mango, peeled and cubed

- 1 tablespoon olive oil

Directions:

1. In a sous vide bag, mix the radishes with the mango and the other ingredients, seal the bag, submerge in the preheated water oven and cook at 185 degrees F for 40 minutes.

2. Divide between plates and serve.

Nutrition: calories 30 fat 1 fiber 0.4 carbs 1 protein 1

42. <u>Creamy Radish and Corn Mix</u>

Preparation time: 10 minutes

Cooking time: 30 minutes

Servings: 4

Ingredients:

- ½ cup heavy cream

- 1 tablespoon butter, melted

- 1 tablespoon green onion, chopped

- 1 tablespoon chives, chopped

- Salt and black pepper to the taste

- ½ pound radishes, halved

- 1 cup corn

Directions:

1. In a sous vide bag, combine the radishes with the corn and the other ingredients, toss, seal the bag, submerge in the preheated water oven and cook at 185 degrees F for 30 minutes.

2. Divide everything between plates and serve as a side dish.

Nutrition: calories 140 fat 23 fiber 3 carbs 6 protein 5

43.   **Balsamic Carrots**

Preparation time: 10 minutes

Cooking time: 30 minutes

Servings: 4

Ingredients:

- 1 pound baby carrots, peeled

- 2 tablespoons olive oil

- 2 tablespoons balsamic vinegar

- 1 teaspoon rosemary, dried

- A pinch of salt and black pepper

- 1 teaspoon chili powder

Directions:

1. In a sous vide bag, mix the carrots with the vinegar and the other ingredients, seal and cook in the water oven at 170 degrees F for 30 minutes.

2. Divide between plates and serve.

Nutrition: calories 149 fat 5 fiber 3 carbs 33 protein 4

44.   <u>Creamy Corn</u>

Preparation time: 10 minutes

Cooking time: 20 minutes

Servings: 2

Ingredients:

- ½ teaspoon turmeric powder

- A pinch of salt and black pepper

- 1 tablespoon cilantro, chopped

- 2 cups fresh corn

- 2 spring onions, chopped

- ½ cup heavy cream

Directions:

1. In a sous vide bag, mix the corn with the cream and the other ingredients, seal the bag, submerge in the water oven and cook at 165 degrees F for 20 minutes.

2. Divide the mix between plates and serve as a side dish.

Nutrition: calories 293 fat 19 fiber 2 carbs 28 protein 6

45.   Rosemary Broccoli Mix

Preparation time: 10 minutes

Cooking time: 30 minutes

Servings: 4

Ingredients:

- 1 pound broccoli florets

- 1 tablespoon avocado oil

- 2 scallions, chopped

- Juice of 1 lime

- 1 tablespoon rosemary, chopped

- 1 tablespoon coriander powder

- 1 tablespoon chives, chopped

- A pinch of salt and black pepper

Directions:

1. In a sous vide bag, mix the broccoli with the oil, scallions and the other ingredients, seal the bag and cook in the water oven and cook at 160 degrees F for 30 minutes.

2. Divide the mix between plates and serve as a side dish.

Nutrition: calories 168 fat 12 fiber 6 carbs 14 protein 5

46.   Creamy Tomatoes

Preparation time: 10 minutes

Cooking time: 20 minutes

Servings: 2

Ingredients:

- ½ teaspoon chili powder

- ¼ cup heavy cream

- A pinch of salt and black pepper

- 1 tablespoon dill, chopped

- 4 scallions, chopped

- 1 tablespoon avocado oil

- 1 pound cherry tomatoes, halved

Directions:

1. In a sous vide bag, mix the tomatoes with the scallions and the other ingredients, seal the bag and cook in the water oven at 165 degrees F for 20 minutes.

2. Divide the mix between plates and serve.

Nutrition: calories 122 fat 7 fiber 3 carbs 10 protein 4

47.   Hot Cauliflower

Preparation time: 10 minutes

Cooking time: 20 minutes

Servings: 4

Ingredients:

- 1 tablespoon avocado oil

- 1 teaspoon chili powder

- Juice of 1 lime

- 1 red chili pepper, chopped

- 1 pound cauliflower florets

- 2 garlic cloves, minced

- A pinch of salt and black pepper

- ½ teaspoon turmeric powder

- ½ teaspoon red pepper flakes, crushed

Directions:

1. In a sous vide bag, mix the cauliflower with the oil, chili and the other ingredients, toss, seal the bag and cook in the water oven at 170 degrees F for 20 minutes.

2. Divide between plates and serve as a side dish.

Nutrition: calories 166 fat 13 fiber 3 carbs 9.6 protein 5

48.   Ginger Green Beans

Preparation time: 10 minutes

Cooking time: 25 minutes

Servings: 4

Ingredients:

- 1 tablespoon avocado oil

- 1 red chili pepper, minced

- 1 tablespoon ginger, grated

- 2 garlic cloves, minced

- Salt and black pepper to the taste

- 1 tablespoon cilantro, chopped

- 2 cups green beans, trimmed and halved

- 1 tablespoon lemon zest, grated

- 1 tablespoon balsamic vinegar

Directions:

1. In a sous vide bag, mix the green beans with the vinegar, lemon zest and the other ingredients, seal the bag, submerge in the water oven and cook at 160 degrees F for 25 minutes.

2. Divide the mix between plates and serve as a side dish.

Nutrition: calories 256 fat 14 fiber 5 carbs 15 protein 5

49. Chives Potatoes

Preparation time: 10 minutes

Cooking time: 30 minutes

Servings: 2

Ingredients:

- 2 tablespoons butter, melted

- 1 pound gold potatoes, peeled and cut into wedges

- 2 tablespoons balsamic vinegar

- A pinch of salt and black pepper

- 1 tablespoon chives, chopped

Directions:

1. In a sous vide bag, mix the potatoes with the melted butter and the other ingredients, seal the bag and cook in the water oven and cook at 180 degrees F for 30 minutes.

2. Divide between plates and serve as a side dish.

Nutrition: calories 152 fat 4 fiber 4 carbs 12 protein 5.3

50.   **Black Beans Mix**

Preparation time: 5 minutes

Cooking time: 20 minutes

Servings: 4

Ingredients:

- 2 cups canned black beans, drained and rinsed

- 1 tablespoon coriander, chopped

- 2 tablespoons butter, soft

- 1 tablespoon balsamic vinegar

- 1 tablespoon chives, chopped

- A pinch of salt and white pepper

Directions:

1. In a sous vide bag, mix the beans with the coriander and the other ingredients, toss, seal the bag and cook in the water oven at 170 degrees F for 20 minutes.

2. Divide between plates and serve as a side dish.

Nutrition: calories 170 fat 6 fiber 3 carbs 22 protein 5

51. Dill Peas

Preparation time: 10 minutes

Cooking time: 25 minutes

Servings: 2

Ingredients:

- ½ teaspoon rosemary, dried
- 1 teaspoon turmeric powder
- A pinch of salt and black pepper
- 1 tablespoon dill, chopped
- 1 tablespoon olive oil
- 2 cups green peas
- Juice of 1 lime

Directions:

1. In a sous vide bag, mix the peas with the oil, lime juice and the other ingredients, toss, seal the bag and cook in the water oven at 150 degrees F for 25 minutes.

2. Divide the mix between plates and serve as a side dish,

Nutrition: calories 220 fat 15 fiber 4 carbs 18 protein 4

CPSIA information can be obtained
at www.ICGtesting.com
Printed in the USA
BVHW060742220321
603170BV00005B/937